Calling

A comedy in one act

Colin and Mary Crowther

Samuel French — London
www.samuelfrench-london.co.uk

Copyright © 2010 by Colin and Mary Crowther
All Rights Reserved

CALLING is fully protected under the copyright laws of the British Commonwealth, including Canada, the United States of America, and all other countries of the Copyright Union. All rights, including professional and amateur stage productions, recitation, lecturing, public reading, motion picture, radio broadcasting, television and the rights of translation into foreign languages are strictly reserved.

ISBN 978-0-573-03387-2

www.samuelfrench.co.uk
www.samuelfrench.com

For Amateur Production Enquiries

United Kingdom and World excluding North America

plays@samuelfrench.co.uk
020 7255 4302/01

Each title is subject to availability from Samuel French, depending upon country of performance.

CAUTION: Professional and amateur producers are hereby warned that CALLING is subject to a licensing fee. Publication of this play does not imply availability for performance. Both amateurs and professionals considering a production are strongly advised to apply to the appropriate agent before starting rehearsals, advertising, or booking a theatre. A licensing fee must be paid whether the title is presented for charity or gain and whether or not admission is charged.

The Professional Rights to this play are controlled by Samuel French Ltd, 24-32 Stephenson Way, London NW1 2HD.

No one shall make any changes in this title for the purpose of production. No part of this book may be reproduced, stored in a retrieval system, or transmitted in any form, by any means, now known or yet to be invented, including mechanical, electronic, photocopying, recording, videotaping, or otherwise, without the prior written permission of the publisher. No one shall upload this title, or part of this title, to any social media websites.

The right of Colin and Mary Crowther to be identified as author of this work has been asserted in accordance with Section 77 of the Copyright, Designs and Patents Act 1988.

CHARACTERS

Kat, truculent, caring
Ann, too eager to please
Caro, restless, rootless
Robyn, ambitious, impatient
Patricia, friendly, sensible
Stephanie, mature, withdrawn

The action takes place in and around an old boarding school one summer weekend

PRODUCTION NOTES

The characters in this play are probably all in their 20's but could be between 17 and 35, making it equally ideal for older teenagers or for a mixed-age cast. Very full stage directions and character descriptions are given to help less experienced groups. But please feel free to do it your own way. All the characters were asked to dress comfortably. None of them has met before so they weren't able to confer. Some thought the instruction was a trick and have dressed formally. So Robyn looks stunning in a top of the range suit, made up to the nines, her hair worn up, as becomes a flight attendant; Caro looks equally formal, but on a tight budget, in the dark suit she probably wears in her work as a hotel receptionist. She also wears make-up and has paid some attention, not very successfully, to her hair. Ann never knows what to wear and looks so old-fashioned her father must have chosen that dull dress and white cardigan for her. Her hair is curly, reinforcing the impression that she is younger than her real age. No make-up, her father wouldn't approve. Kat, cherishing her role as rebel, is a Goth – not caring how out of date, or out of place, it might look. But she is clearly not comfortable with that image in this place and each time she leaves the stage, she returns with one less extreme decoration, one more attempt at toning it all down, especially the make-up. Patricia and Stephanie are the only ones who look really comfortable, Patricia in a favourite top, warm cardigan and skirt, Stephanie smarter in new clothes: a plain white T-shirt, pastel tracksuit and white trainers, all chosen, one suspects, to make her look younger and not stand out. She and Kat are the only ones to wear a crucifix, though it's difficult to tell if Kat's isn't part of her Goth image.

Enjoy!

Colin and Mary Crowther

CHARACTERISATION NOTES

Kat is bristling. Whenever she meets new people, her low self-esteem means that her hackles go up and her claws come out: scarred by life, her first defence is attack. A pity. She is intelligent, amusing, dedicated, caring, perceptive and painfully honest, but always being hurt because she comes across as aggressive and takes the huff at the slightest provocation

Ann is nervous, younger than her years and desperate to please, to belong. But what she says is certainly not what she rehearsed with her father. We soon begin to wonder if this is really the too-dutiful daughter or the ultimate, if unconscious, act of self-defence... In which case, is she stupid, or very clever or very, very sly? Whatever the truth, we feel we want to protect her

As **Caro** herself recognizes, there is something lacking in her and this insecurity results in her constantly seeking approbation. Perhaps this can be traced back to her childhood: both her parents were in the army and she rarely saw them. She was sent to a boarding school and in the holidays to the care of her doting grandmother. If she could only find a friend who would value her and raise her self-confidence, then perhaps the little girl would finally blossom and mature. It's what she seeks in this job, but it will come at a price she is not yet able or willing to pay

Robyn is impatient for change and for the chance to lead that change. The youngest child - by far - of a family of high-fliers, she has always struggled to be noticed; to be taken seriously. The trouble is - or perhaps it is her saving grace - that she is so transparently ambitious and ruthless in pursuit of that ambition. She's a hard nut to crack, but remember that hardness is just her shell

Patricia is remarkably relaxed for someone facing so important a weekend. This is because she is certain of her calling, but it does help to reveal what a friendly and sensible person she is. She's certainly the sort of person we all want as our best friend, because she listens all the time. Consequently, she can sum people up quickly. Miraculously, even then, she seems prepared to accept everyone as they are. But underneath her confidence lurks a very real fear

Stephanie at first seems aloof, guarded, occasionally impatient and irritable, but as she changes and grows, these clouds lift and she is revealed in her final interview with the panel as a mature woman, at peace with herself

Other plays by Colin and Mary Crowther, published by Samuel French Ltd:

Footprints in the Sand (Colin Crowther)
Just Passing
Noah's Ark (for children)
Reflections
Till We Meet Again
Tryst (Colin Crowther)
An Untimely Frost (formerly The Lost Garden)

*With our gratejul thanks to Joyce
Kirkman LGSM, an inspiring teacher
and dear friend, for her invaluable
help and support*

CALLING

The setting is very simple: eight identical chairs in a wide semi-circle, right across the centre of the stage, each facing DC. There is a small table ULC. On the table are notebooks, pens and four A4 buff envelopes, each one containing a typed sheet of instructions and a fifth one for their solutions. Offstage right is a long, strong, old plank

The action alternates between interview sections and group sessions. For the interview sections, everyone sits alertly focusing on the interview panel, who are assumed to be DC. They usually sit in the same order for the interview sections. From SR: Kat, space, Ann, Caro, Robyn, space, Patricia, Stephanie. In the group sessions, they visibly relax and revert to their real selves

Lights snap on to reveal a band of cold, bright light across C: this is the interview lighting

Kat I don't. It's the last job on earth I want. But it's got my name on it. Like nursing did. E.M.I... What? ...Oh, Elderly Mentally Infirm... What I'm doing now. People with dementia. No one else wants to... Fine. I'll do it. And I love it. Love them. Good job I do. No one else will. And now this.

Ann Couldn't get plainer than that.

Caro Ooh, that's a hard one. I'll have to think about that.

Robyn You see what I mean? Sweet people. But frankly, misfits and losers. You see a lot of that in my profession.

Ann Nursery Nurse.

Caro Hotel Receptionist... Well, I was. Before that, Home Carer. Old people. Not very nice old people...
Robyn Flight attendant. Senior Flight Attendant.
Patricia Teacher... Secondary... Science...
Stephanie You know what I do. What I want to know is why I'm here.
Caro Before that, sales assistant... Supermarket... Stacking shelves. Boring.
Robyn London, New York, Paris, Rome. Like the perfume. (*She laughs*)
Caro Before that, hairdresser... Well, brushing up after the hairdresser. Really boring.
Robyn Management, really.
Caro I don't think I've got any strengths, not as such, but tell me what to do, stick me at the back, you'd hardly know I'm here.
Stephanie I still don't know why I'm here.
Patricia Because this is where I'm meant to be.
Ann It would make Father so proud.
Kat (*rising*) Oh, let's stop wasting each other's time. I know you'll reject me. Came expecting it... (*Moving behind her chair, as if to exit, then turning back*) When you do?
Patricia Turn me down? I hadn't thought...
Kat I'll find someone else who feels rejected... Look after them. Because I know how they feel. (*She turns to face upstage and freezes*)
Ann (*rising*) So proud. (*Moving behind her chair, as if to exit*) What do I think? Don't you see? This isn't about me. (*She turns upstage and freezes*)
Robyn (*rising and moving behind her chair*) Who knows? In ten years, I could be sitting there. Interviewing you! (*She laughs nervously, turns upstage and freezes*)
Caro Oh, yes, I have got a strength. Knew I must have, somewhere. (*Rising and moving behind her chair*) I can start tomorrow. (*She turns to face upstage and freezes*)
Patricia (*rising slowly*) If you turn me down, I'll go away.

Go back to my classroom, to my teaching. (*Appearing to give up she moves behind her chair, then looks up and smiles*) Next year, I'll come back. And I'll keep coming back. Till what's calling me is calling you. (*She turns upstage and freezes*)

Stephanie (*remaining stubbornly seated*) Will someone please tell me what this is all about!

Quick cross fade to general lighting over the whole stage

Stephanie crosses her legs but otherwise remains sitting, nursing her thoughts. Patricia crosses to the table and looks at what is on it. Caro and Robyn stand to one side near the back of the room, talking quietly to each other. Ann wants to belong, but doesn't know where

Kat (*flopping down in her chair*) Weird.

The others look at her, then look away

Patricia It's all here. Paper, pens, the dreaded envelopes.
Ann Oh, good. Isn't it?
Robyn Frankly? I'm less than impressed.
Caro I must admit, I was disappointed — when they told us to come here, to a boarding school. I thought we'd be going to — oh, what did they tell us to call it? — HQ.
Kat Weird.
Robyn And last night? When we arrived?
Ann That was odd — no one to greet us — school holidays, of course, but there must have been someone here because ——
Robyn A scribbled note and a bag of groceries — not what I call hospitality.
Ann I was surprised we had to cook our own meals.
Caro Make our own beds!
Kat Weird.
Robyn And those rules — about what we could and could not

say —— the words we could use.
Ann "Job".
Caro "HQ".
Ann "Shiftwork".
Robyn And today it gets worse. They give us four tasks — all weekend to complete them — then don't stick round to see how we get on.
Patricia Still, better get started.
Robyn I think we should start by introducing ourselves. Last night's a bit hazy...

Kat and Stephanie groan audibly, then smile at each other, recognizing rebel kinship

Everyone comes and sits down in interview sequence, except Patricia, who remains standing by the table, the first envelope in her hand. They look in front of them, addressing the panel

Quick cross fade to interview lighting

Kat Kat. Not Katherine, Katrina, Katya, Katy, Kate or Kay. Kat.
Ann Ann. Just plain Ann. Can't get plainer than that.
Caro Caro. Short for Caroline. In Italian, it means Beloved. Not that anyone's ever called me that in Italian. Or even English.
Robyn Robyn. With a Y.
Patricia Patricia. Pat... Whatever.
Stephanie Stephanie. Sounds strange, after all these...
Kat Why don't they just get on with it!

Quick cross fade to general lighting

Call us in, one by one, ask us all they want, and then... let us go. Instead ——
Robyn Instead they call us in, one at a time, ask one silly

question, then call us back and ask another.
Patricia I'm sure they have their reasons.
Stephanie I'm beginning to doubt it.
Robyn It's so unsophisticated. When I had my interview at B.A. —

Kat groans, as if in real pain

They had this whole battery of tests, designed to weed out the — shall we say? — unstable.
Kat Did it work?
Patricia (*stepping forward quickly; opening the envelope and reading aloud*) Task One: "You are out walking on your own when suddenly you come across a man who has fallen into quicksand. Already it is up to his shoulders. Soon he will drown. What would you do?"
Caro I thought they'd start with something easy.
Stephanie I think they did.
Ann I know! I'd step back. In case I fell in. Are they all going to be this easy?
Caro That's a good idea.
Stephanie Do we have to agree? On our answer?
Robyn Maybe we're like a jury. We need a foreman, to count the vote, summarize the pros and cons, persuade the dithering. I don't mind volunteering... (*She rises, not expecting any opposition*)
Patricia It says, "you are on your own". So no, I don't think we need a foreman.
Kat Pity.

Robyn sits, miffed. Inspiration strikes Ann, not that anyone notices

Ann Oh! I've seen this somewhere.
Robyn I'll go first, shall I?
Stephanie I think Ann already has.

Robyn I'd call air-sea rescue.
Caro That is a good idea!
Stephanie But you're on your own.
Robyn I never go anywhere without my mobile.
Ann It was in a film. About a nun.
Patricia Caro, what would you do?
Caro I'd run for help. Get someone responsible.
Stephanie No time. It's already up to his neck.
Ann Audrey Hepburn!
Robyn You seem to know all the answers, Stephanie. What would you do?
Stephanie (*shrugs*) I'd start by throwing him the lifebelt.
Caro He could pull you in. Then you'd both drown.
Robyn What if there isn't a lifebelt?
Stephanie There's always a lifebelt. Stands to reason. If there's quicksand, there's a warning. And a lifebelt. Help him out, if I could. If not, pour him a coffee — feed him a sandwich — keep his energy up.
Caro What for?
Stephanie So we can talk through why he decided to kill himself.
Caro But it was an accident! Wasn't it?
Ann It's a bit morbid. Couldn't they think up something nicer? With babies?
Patricia I've never seen anyone die before. Oh, I'd try to help — smile, take messages, listen, say... whatever — but I know, when it came to the end, I'd look away.
Ann (*jumping up*) Yes! That's it. You listen to his confession!
Robyn You're not a priest.
Ann And smile. So as he sinks, gurgling in his final agony, he'd have something beautiful to look at. Me. (*She sinks back into her chair, dramatically*)
Kat Audrey Hepburn. *A Nun's Story*.
Ann That's right! Trouble is, I think she got it wrong.
Robyn So we're agreed. Caroline —
Caro Caro.

Robyn Sweet. Caro came closest. To me. I'd organize air-sea rescue, ambulance, that sort of thing. Stephanie threw in a lifebelt and a sandwich. Shall we vote on it?
Kat He's about to drown — not go on a picnic!
Robyn Very well. What would you do, Kat?
Kat Simple. I'd hit him on the head. Knock him out. Then at least he wouldn't know he was drowning.

Horrified pause, then slowly the others see the funny side

Robyn Ah, Kat and her wicked sense of humour.

But their laughter has backed Kat into a corner. And a cornered cat will do just one thing...

Kat (*rising*) Who's joking?
Robyn (*to Patricia*) What's next?
Kat (*flaring*) I'm a nurse. What do you expect me to do? I'm there to kill the pain.
Stephanie But pain can be useful.
Kat Huh! If you think that, you haven't seen pain — not real pain. Oh, for God's sake! It's what they want. Patients. Relatives. Kill the pain.
Stephanie (*carefully*) Is that what you do? When your patients are in too much pain? Kill them?
Kat Course not. You stay with them. Hold their hand. Wipe their brow. And in the deep dark bowels of the night, reach out your hand... (*Chickening out*)... and go, "There, there." (*Pause*) I need a cigarette.

Kat exits DR, *pulling out her cigarettes as she goes*

Ann (*rising*) I'm really hungry now.
Caro Oh, so am I!
Robyn It's only half past eleven.
Stephanie What about Task Two?

Ann Couldn't we have an early lunch? To give us energy for the next one? Something tells me we're going to need it.
Caro Good idea.

Patricia rises

Robyn Perhaps we should all stretch our legs. (*She rises and heads* DR)

Caro and Ann rise. Caro starts to follow Robyn, but Ann is not yet sure whom to follow

Patricia I'll get it, shall I? Sandwiches OK? (*She turns* US, *heading for* UL)
Stephanie (*jumping up and intercepting her; trying to put her off*) I'll do it.
Patricia You made dinner last night. Least I can do is make a few ——
Stephanie You did the washing up. Let me — please.
Robyn We need a rota. Ensure no one gets imposed on. I'll do that. I'm good at rotas.
Ann What can I do?
Patricia (*to Ann*) The washing up?

Patricia exits UL

Stephanie (*looking defeated then realizing her behaviour is attracting attention*) I'll just... write up our answers... to Task One... Someone should... (*She turns her chair* US *and sits at the table and begins to write*)
Robyn But you could cheat.
Stephanie Why should I want to?
Robyn Sweet. In that case, I'm off to explore.
Caro What was that all about?
Robyn Dark horse, our Stephanie. What do we know about her?

Caro Last night, after dinner, when we were all chatting in the Common Room, where was she? And this morning, she didn't show for breakfast.
Ann (*joining them* DR) Had hers early. She said.
Robyn Where does she get to?
Ann She's taking time out.
Robyn Like a gap year?
Ann More of a sabbatical, I think.
Caro From what?

Kat enters DR. *She herds the others back to their seats*

Kat They want us back in.
Robyn Oh, really! What for this time?

They resume their seats for an interview session, all except Stephanie and Patricia

Quick cross fade to interview lighting

Kat Family? Haven't got any.
Robyn I can't wait to see their faces!
Kat When I was little, my mother used to tell me a story, how, when she knew she couldn't have any children, she went to this big, long room, with rows and rows of babies. And chose me. I loved that story. Made me feel special.
Ann Oh, they're all in favour. Not my sister. She thinks I'm a fool. But she doesn't live at home now. Nor does Mother... I haven't seen her since... So Father pinned all his hopes on me — and he has such high hopes of people. Till they let him down. And everyone does, in the end. My sister...Mother... But the Head at my old school — ever so nice, I had a chat with her, just like this — she said I had to try something else first. So I did. Nursery Nurse. And I love it. But now Father thinks the time is right. And he would be so proud...
Kat As I grew older, I'd get into mischief — nothing more —

tell a fib, break something — she told a different story. How, if I was bad, she would take me back — choose another, better, little girl. Leave me behind in that big, long room, with rows and rows of other, bad little girls...
Caro No close family. We're... a bit scattered, always have been. But friends, that's a different story... Best friend? No. Not at the moment. People come and go, don't they? But the way I see it, with you, I'd have hundreds of best friends... Twenty-three? Oh. Well, twenty-three's... nice... One would be nice.
Kat Moral to her story? Love is something you must earn. And I'd never be good enough. So I grew frantic, desperate to please. But no, try as I might, I kept doing something wrong... And every night, the shadow of that long, dark room reached out for me...
Ann What do I think? Don't you see? It isn't about me.
Kat So no. No family.

Patricia enters UL, with plate of sandwiches

Patricia They think I'm crazy. But I can tell, they're not surprised, not one bit.
Ann (*rising; shaking, clearly very distressed*) Can I go now? Please.

Quick cross fade to general lighting

Caro takes Ann's hand, leads her UC. Robyn and Kat eye each other, then ignore each other

Patricia (*thrusting the sandwiches under Stephanie's nose, preventing her from working*) Sandwich, Stephanie?
Stephanie Oh, I...
Patricia After all, you made them.
Stephanie Sorry.
Patricia Why, Stephanie?

Stephanie I didn't think anyone else would want to...
Patricia Well, think again. We're all in this together. Or supposed to be. It's share and share alike from now on. Agreed?

Stephanie nods

You did the meal last night. And breakfast. And lunch. I'll do it tonight. Someone else can do it tomorrow.
Stephanie And Robyn can write up the rota.

They laugh. Patricia takes the plate to Robyn

Robyn I don't eat lunch.

Patricia places the plate on the chair beside Robyn

Stephanie I've got a problem.
Patricia And I wish you'd talk about it.
Stephanie I've written up the ideas we had, but I can't remember who said what...

As each person's name is mentioned, they take a sandwich, except Patricia and Stephanie

Patricia Try me.
Stephanie Robyn —
Patricia With a Y.
Robyn Oh, cheese. Perhaps just one...
Stephanie She would call in the professionals.
Patricia Never be without your mobile.
Stephanie Ann —
Ann Is that lunch?
Stephanie Ann thinks she's Audrey Hepburn.
Ann My favourite. Food.
Stephanie Who's the one having second thoughts?

Patricia Interesting. You got that impression, too. Her name's Caroline.
Caro (*to Ann*) Oh, no. I'm sure. Well, quite sure. You can never be totally sure until you've done it, can you? Trouble is, by then, it's too late. You've gone too far... I had that trouble with a boyfriend once... (*She sits beside Robyn*)

Kat rises, goes over and takes the plate from them then goes back to her corner and sits, eating slowly

Patricia Kat thinks she's the Terminator.
Stephanie Then there's you.
Patricia Patricia
Stephanie The one who'd look away.
Patricia The coward.
Stephanie (*shaking her head*) I suspect the only honest one among us.
Patricia And you. The practical one. All there with the lifebelt. And the sandwiches. Dead giveaway, those sandwiches.
Stephanie Still... someone...
Robyn Missing.
Caro Sometimes I think there's something missing in —
Robyn They're in there, we're out here... so why do I feel they can see every move we make; hear every word we say?

Everyone stops eating and starts thinking

Ann They use spies in MFI.
Caro You mean — one of us?
Kat MFI?
Robyn A spy!
Ann Oh. Silly me. Not MFI. I meant MI5.
Robyn (*to herself*) That's it! The place is bugged!

Quick cross fade to interview lighting

Calling 13

Everyone leaves the stage, Kat taking the sandwiches with her

Only Caro and Robyn remain. They are being interviewed at different times so do not react to each other

Caro Strengths? Me?
Robyn Weaknesses? Me?
Caro Oh. "What strengths would I bring to your organization?" That's a hard one. I'll have to think about that.
Robyn (*trying her famous silvery laugh, but a quick look at the panel shows her she must take this seriously*) No, no, what I mean... Let me see. What do I mean?
Caro Nearly there.
Robyn Gosh. Where to start? It won't be that I'm not willing. I am. Very. Or that I don't get on with people. I do. But I know where to draw the line. You need that in my line of work. With the airline. Especially in Business Class. Take a man above twelve thousand feet and his hands... I told him, "I'm not part of the duty-frees". Then I... And he... (*She lapses into painful memories and for the first time looks human and very vulnerable*)
Caro Ready now. My strengths are... I'm a hotel receptionist at the moment, or was, so I'm used to shift work, including nights, wearing uniform, smiling, getting on with people...I like a uniform. It's one less thing to worry about. Leaves me free to worry about everything else.
Robyn How did I feel?
Caro What else? I take things in, ever so quick. They don't always stick, though, not first time.
Robyn Like a lump of meat. I wonder if that's why I became a vegetarian: I know how it feels to be the meat.
Caro Come to think of it — I mean, really think — I don't think I've got any strengths, not as such. Sorry.
Robyn Sorry. Where were we? Oh, yes, your weakness. Don't tell me. You're finding it harder and harder to find the right

people. Management material.
Caro I think there's something missing. Inside me. I don't know... like a mint, with a hole in the middle.
Robyn You see what I mean? Sweet people. And one feels for them. But frankly, misfits and losers. You see a lot of that in my profession. Flight attendant. Transatlantic. Heathrow-New York, that sort of thing. Management, really.
Caro (*rising*) But stick me at the back, tell me what to do, you won't know I'm here. (*She moves behind her chair*)
Robyn And that's where I think I could be so useful. After a period of, shall we say, basic training, I thought, secondment to a university, degree programme, then overseas placement, Paris, Rome...
Caro Oh, yes! I have got a strength. Knew I must have. Somewhere.
Robyn (*rising and moving behind her chair*) Who knows? In ten years, I could be sitting there. Interviewing you!
Caro I can start tomorrow.

Robyn emits her practised silvery laugh

Quick cross fade to general lighting

Stephanie and Patricia enter UL, *Ann* UR, *Kat* DR

Stephanie Let's get on, shall we?

Murmurs of assent. Stephanie opens Envelope Two

Robyn You were in there a long time. How did it go?
Caro Wonderful! They're so *simpatico*. You can tell them anything!
Robyn I hope you didn't.

They all meet C

Stephanie (*reading aloud*) Task two. "In groups of four, build a human pyramid".
Kat Is that it?
Patricia But there aren't enough of us.
Stephanie Four... Why four?
Robyn It's obvious. They got it wrong. Two teams of three is what they mean. Who wants to be on my team?
Caro (*jumping up and down*) Me! Me!
Ann (*shy, but determined*) Me.
Kat (*stepping forward with a sinister smile*) And me.
Robyn Ah. I choose — Oh, who? Who? — Caro. Ann.
Kat Shucks.
Robyn Sorry, Katy. Another time?

Kat growls

Ann Perhaps they want us to share. One of us helps one of them, then one of them helps one of us... Perhaps.

They ignore her

Caro Where shall we go?
Robyn My team over here — now!

They're off, gathering in a huddle, DL. *After a quick, whispered explanation from Robyn, they start searching. Robyn examines on and under the table, while the other two, on hands and knees, look under the chairs* SL, *then, still on all fours, begin to examine the floor, gradually working* DS

Stephanie What are they doing?
Kat They think the place is bugged.
Stephanie Pathetic!
Kat Is it?
Stephanie Why ask me?
Kat You look like you've been here before.

Stephanie Never.
Kat Cross your heart and hope to —
Stephanie Honest injun.
Kat (*taking out her cigarettes*) Anyone got a light?
Patricia No.
Stephanie There are some matches under the sink.
Kat See?
Patricia What is it about a school? You put six grown women back in school and in less than a day they've regressed to fifteen year olds!
Kat Absolutely. OK, gang. Who wants to be on my team?

Patricia springs up; Stephanie jumps up and down: two of the gawkiest thirteen year old rejects ever to disgrace a playing field

Patricia Me!
Stephanie Me! Me!
Kat I choose...

Patricia shoves Stephanie out of the way to be first in the queue

... you and you. Bagsy — here!

They gather UR

Ann Caro, what does a hidden microphone look like?

Caro shrugs. They work on. Robyn sits in a chair, SL, *deep in thought*

Kat A pyramid. Remind me. How many sides?
Stephanie Should be four.
Patricia Can be three.
Kat That's lucky.
Patricia I think the key will be to get the base right.

Calling

They practise creating the base of a pyramid. Ann and Caro give up

Ann We should be getting on.
Caro What's the point? If there's no one to watch us — check who does what — how will they know we did anything?
Ann You think we're wasting our time?
Caro Or filling in time. Maybe what matters is how we do in the interview. Maybe these tasks are just to stop us getting bored? You know, like in school, when the teacher nipped out for a bit.

The other group creates the base by standing in a triangle with toes touching

Stephanie Now for the sides.
Caro Robyn, have you seen the time?
Robyn Hush! I'm thinking.

The other group creates the sides by facing into each other

Got it!
Ann I thought —
Robyn No need. I know just what to do — (*She stands in a basic triangle shape, arms together, reaching skywards*)
Caro What do we do?
Robyn Crouch. At my feet. Either side.
Ann Pardon?
Robyn Like those thingummies — Egyptian thingummies — animals.

Ann mouths "dogs?" Caro shrugs. Obediently they go down on all fours on either side of her. Meanwhile, the other group shoots their hands together into the air and leans inwards. Result? A perfect triangular-based pyramid. Ann and Caro, on a barked command from Robyn, go back on their haunches, paws in the air, panting, like performing poodles

Stephanie ⎫
Robyn   ⎭ (*together*) Perfect!

Kat Oh, Robyn! You are — Look! Stephanie! Isn't she just — ?

They both break out laughing, leaning against the chairs

Patricia Oh, behave, you two!

Too late, they are helpless with laughter and sit. Robyn, hurt, has a huff and marches c, where she sits in her chair

Caro (*going on the attack*) That's right. Laugh. It's easy to laugh at her. Because she's an idiot.
Robyn Who?
Caro She gets on my nerves, too. And if she mentions that poxy airline again, I'll strangle her myself.
Robyn You?
Caro She thinks she'll get in because she's better than us. But we all know she's an idiot.
Robyn Me?
Caro But is that all she is? You want an idiot? Take Ann. She thinks she'll get in by doing what everyone tells her. Whereas we all know you don't get anything like that. Except dizzy.
Ann Oh. If you say so.
Caro But is that what she really thinks?
Kat I wondered that.
Caro Did you, Kat? Did you also wonder if you're an even bigger idiot? You think no one will want you anyway, so you set out to prove yourself right. And you only succeed in proving them right. What's behind that, then?
Patricia Yes, why do you do that?
Kat (*shrugs*) Saves time.
Caro And you, Steph. You want in, but only on your terms. Why? What makes you so sure you know it all? But look who's talking. I want in on any terms! Which makes me the

biggest idiot of all!
Stephanie I feel thoroughly ashamed.
Patricia I feel left out. What's wrong with me?
Kat I'll tell you later.
Caro Look behind the mask, that's what I mean. See the person underneath. Try to understand why.
Ann (*turning* DS) And I thought we were all getting on so well.

Caro sits L of Robyn. Ann rises and makes for the extreme SL seat

Robyn Nice to know who your friends are.
Caro You haven't got any. You've got me. And I — God help me — have got you. Think about it. Want to swap?
Robyn (*meekly*) No.
Kat Right, that settles it. I shall love that bitch if it kills her. (*She marches over and sits beside Robyn. Brainwave. She gets out her cigarettes*) Cigarette?
Robyn (*getting out her lighter*) Light?

They smile and start chatting, pocketing their goodies for later

Ann Patricia? (*No reply*) Patricia?
Patricia Not now, Ann.
Ann I don't want to be here.
Patricia Then why did you come?
Ann Father...
Patricia Do you do everything that man says?
Ann In the end.
Patricia But it's your life!
Ann Doesn't feel like it.
Patricia Oh, Ann, Ann!
Ann I am trying. I flunked my interview. I played stupid at all the games.
Patricia Tasks.
Ann They felt like games to me. Trouble is, it's not working. Everyone else is so hopeless, they're just as likely to take me

on as the best of a bad lot.
Patricia Oh, thank you!
Ann I've done it all my life. The only way I could stand up to Father was to play stupid, then when I'm cornered, agree, and try to make a mess of it. (*Pause*) Patricia? (*Pause*)
Patricia Yes?
Ann Have you got a boyfriend?
Patricia I had, once.
Ann Did you love him?
Patricia We were engaged.
Ann Mine's called Bernie. We work at the same nursery. He makes me laugh... What happened? To your boyfriend?
Patricia I broke it off.
Ann How sad!
Patricia (*thinking about this and suddenly realizing*) No. I realized I loved someone else more. (*And this gives her back the courage and sense of purpose she needs. She returns to her seat*)
Ann I'm not sure I do. Not sure I can. Oh, decisions, decisions!

Quick cross fade to interview lighting

Stephanie (*hurrying back to her seat*) No!
Patricia If you turn me down? Gosh! I hadn't thought... What would I do if you...
Kat Knew it!
Robyn Not you as well!
Caro But where will I go?
Ann You can't! I've got to get in! I've got to!
Kat (*rising and moving behind her chair*) Oh, let's stop wasting each other's time. I know you'll reject me. Came expecting it... What will I do?
Patricia But of course, this has to be right for both of us. So, where would I go? (*She rises and moves behind her chair*)
Caro Where will I go?

Ann I've got to stay! Please! I couldn't bear it if I had to tell him — if I let him down as well!
Kat I'll find someone else who feels rejected. Look after them. Because I know how they feel.
Patricia I'll go away. Go back to my classroom, go on teaching... (*Suddenly smiling*) Next year, I'll come back.
Stephanie But this is my home! I never thought it was. Till you tried to take it away. But it is. All I have. All I want.
Patricia I don't know how else to explain... All my life I've stood on the shore, and watched the others playing in the water, yet I've always known that would never be for me. I was just like them, luckier than many, happier, too. I had a job I loved, a man who loved me, home, friends, health, family. But somehow still on the shore, watching. Then, it came to me. I don't want to be one of the swimmers, but one of the waves that holds them up; part of the tide that washes the world clean, not part of the world that, however hard we try, just keeps making it dirty again... So, if you turn me down, I'll go away. But I'll be back. And I'll keep coming back. Till what's calling me is calling you ... (*Smiling*; *at peace now*) I should warn you. Scientists are very persistent.
Stephanie Enough! I can't go on with this — not any more!

Quick cross fade to general lighting

Kat runs over to Stephanie and kneels, concerned, in front of her, holding her hands. Robyn rises and walks behind Caro's and Ann's chairs

Patricia (*to Kat and Stephanie*) I've been thinking.
Robyn (*to Caro and Ann*) Great news.
Caro Who for?
Robyn Think. Task Two : In groups of four.
Caro But there's only six of us.
Robyn Exactly. Eight chairs. Six people. Two didn't turn up! At least. And of those who are left, well, I ask you! The odds

in our favour are rising all the time! (*She nods in the direction of the other group*)

Ann and Caro follow her gaze. Robyn crosses to the table and picks up Envelope Three, a pad and pen

Patricia I've been thinking. Maybe there are so few of us here today, not because no one else was interested, no one else applied, but because they're holding lots of weekends like this, all year, all over the country.
Kat Around the world. Robyn said they have HQs in Europe and America.
Stephanie Africa, too.
Kat Really?
Patricia So maybe there are lots of us, being looked at in really small groups, so they can look really hard.
Kat I wish they'd hurry up and get it over with.
Robyn Ready, everyone?
Patricia (*to Kat and Stephanie*) Now behave, you two.
Kat Yes, Robyn.
Robyn Good. Task Three. (*She opens the envelope and reads*) "Working as one group, use whatever you can find to build a bridge over an imaginary stream. Then use the bridge to cross the stream. It is important that all of you complete this task." How very odd.

Patricia and Kat exit SR

Stephanie When will they realize? Bigger the group, bigger the problems!
Caro Wonder why this one's so important?
Patricia (*offstage*) Not much inspiration here. Just a load of old boxes.

Kat re-enters, dragging a long plank behind her

Kat And this.
Ann Oh, I thought that had been left by mistake.
Kat I'm beginning to realize — nothing here happens by accident.
Robyn Ideas? Friends?
Stephanie We could put the chairs either side — create, like, banks.
Caro Lie the plank across them, you mean?
Patricia (*backing away; quietly*) Oh, no!
Robyn (*clapping her hands*) Exactly. Come along! No time to waste!
Kat What can I do, Robyn?
Robyn You can be the stream. Lie down. There.
Kat But these are my best —
Robyn Katrina? Do you want to be left out? Again?
Kat No, Robyn. Sorry, Robyn.
Robyn Rest of you — three chairs either side of our raging little stream. Ha, ha!
Kat Ha, ha!
Robyn Plank across.

Everyone jumps to it. It should only take moments to set up the bridge safely with a little practice

   (*Busying herself writing out a list of everyone's names, ready to record who passes or fails*) Now. Who wants to be first?
Caro Me, me!
Kat Can I get up now, please?
Robyn Very well. Caro, show them how it's done.

Caro crosses confidently. Everyone applauds. Patricia is still shrinking back

   Well done, Caro. Now—
Kat Me!
Patricia I can't.

Ann Think of Audrey Hepburn. In *My Fair Lady!*
Robyn Ann.

Ann crosses very nervously. More applause

Stephanie (*to Patricia*) Patricia?
Patricia I can't do it.
Stephanie Do what?
Patricia This. I can't bear it. Heights. And heights over water, worst of all. I'm sorry. I just can't.
Robyn Now...
Kat Me! Me!
Robyn Stephanie.
Stephanie But it's just a couple of chairs with a plank across. Not high at all.
Patricia It is to me.
Robyn Stephanie!
Stephanie Wait!
Patricia Please.
Stephanie I'll help. (*Crossing, then calls across*) Stand on the chair. Now I'll stand on this one, on the other bank. OK?
Patricia (*standing on the chair, taking one step forward, losing courage*) No.
Stephanie Now take my hand.
Patricia I can't!
Stephanie Damn it! Why can't you people do as you're told!
Patricia (*trying, failing, and curling up on her chair*) I'm sorry. So sorry.
Stephanie (*crouching on opposite chair; regretfully*) No. My fault. Oh, I told them! Big groups don't work. It's so much easier, quicker, to do it on your own!
Ann Told who?
Robyn Now you, Patricia.
Caro What's the problem?
Stephanie No good. She's afraid of heights.
Patricia And water.

Calling

Caro But it's not real water. It's only pretend.
Kat Pretend...

This gives Kat an idea. She sits down and starts pulling on imaginary Wellington boots

Patricia Please. Just... count me out.
Ann But it says all of us — using the bridge!
Patricia There are no sides! No rail!
Caro Robyn! Do something!
Robyn Oh, well, five out of six will have to do.
Caro But we all have to—
Robyn We can't all fail because of one weak link.
Ann Maybe — if someone holds me — I could walk out halfway — help her over?
Caro Kat!
Kat Hang on. Just wait till I pull this one on.
Patricia This what?
Kat Can't you see? Wellington boots. Pink. With butterflies.

Patricia giggles

Ooh! Tight fit. Now. Ann? Ready your end?

Ann walks out to halfway, nervously, Stephanie holding her round the waist

Patricia This is silly!
Kat (*wading into the stream, from Patricia's side*) No. This is fun. Down the bank, through the bulrushes. You see? Not deep at all.
Patricia (*rising*) Are you sure?
Kat Just a gentle stream on a warm summer day. Barely up to my ankles. Paddling. That's all I'm doing. Oh, look, a baby trout.
Patricia Where? (*She steps out onto the bridge to see*)

Kat (*offering up her hand*) Hold the rail, please.

Patricia holds Kat's hands and slowly, hesitantly, but no longer fearfully, Patricia begins to cross

And hovering ahead, a kingfisher... called Ann.
Patricia I've always wanted to see a kingfisher!
Kat (*handing her over to Ann*) Well, now you have.

Ann, if truth be told, is even more nervous, having to walk backwards, but she does it, and before Patricia knows it, she has reached the other side

Patricia (*apologetically*) I'm not being silly.
Kat I am.
Ann So am I.
Patricia How much further?
Stephanie You're there.

Patricia is thrilled. They help her down. Stephanie and Ann applaud her. Kat goes back to cross the bridge herself

Seems I was wrong. Bigger the group, the more there are to help.
Ann More fun, too.
Kat (*starting to cross the bridge; getting halfway and pretending to be losing her balance*) Help! Help!
Patricia Oh, don't be such a baby!

So they are all across. Stephanie gives Patricia a big hug. Applause all round. They clear away, stacking the six chairs they have used CR *and replacing the two central chairs. The plank is carted off* SR

Robyn Well done, everyone, full marks! Now clear away, quickly please. Light's fading. (*To Caro*) I've worked it out. Who the spy is.

Caro Stop seeing everyone as rivals — try seeing them as friends.
Robyn Ha! Like who?
Caro Like me! (*She marches to the table*)

Robyn follows her

Stephanie Kat? Are you going to sit there all day?
Kat (*taking off her last boot*) I'm waterlogged. (*She pours water out of it*)

The others laugh

Robyn Caro...? (*She deposits envelope, pad and pen on the table*)
Caro Want to know a secret? A real secret? Everyone got a tick on Task Three.
Robyn I know.
Caro Everyone except you!

Caro exits UL

Robyn grabs her notepad and pores over it. The terrible truth quickly dawns

Patricia (*heading for* UL) I'd better put that chicken on.
Kat (*catching up with her* CS) Oh, but what about my friend?
Robyn Who?
Kat You. You're vegetarian, aren't you?
Robyn Oh, that's all right. I eat chicken.
Stephanie Chicken isn't vegetarian.
Robyn Yes it is. Chickens don't eat meat. So chickens are vegetarian. So I eat chicken. All the time.
Kat Brilliant!
Patricia Chicken it is.

Patricia exits UL

Robyn Sweet of you... to think of me... Katya.
Kat The name's Kat.
Robyn But Katya's nicer.
Kat I don't do nicer.

Robyn shows Kat her cigarette lighter

(*Feeling in her pocket for her cigarettes*) I suppose I could try...
Stephanie (*to Ann*) Come on, you and I can do the vegetables.
Kat (*feeling torn*) Then, I'll wash up. With my new friend Robyn.
Robyn And I'll let you.

Robyn and Kat exit DL

Ann and Stephanie make for UL, *when Ann hears someone calling. She turns and faces out front, listening, then taps Stephanie on the shoulder*

Ann Steph? They want you. No, just you.

Quick cross fade to interview lighting

Ann exits UL

Stephanie is alarmed, then relaxes and smiles. She crosses and sits in the chair, C

Stephanie I think I know this bit. You're coming to each one of us in turn, to ask that final question...

Everyone enters UL *and walks in a line across the back of the stage*

They turn and face out front during Stephanie's line

After everything that has happened this weekend, do you still want to join us? (*She looks up at the panel*)
Patricia Yes. Oh, yes.
Robyn Oh, absolutely.
Kat Not if you're daft enough to want me.
Caro Ye—es... If everyone else does...
Ann (*in a small voice*) No.
Stephanie Yes, I'm ready. (*She rises to go*)

Everyone else freezes through this Scene, but Stephanie hears the panel ask her something else. She sits and thinks

If you'd asked me a week ago — even yesterday — I'd have told you all this living together — it just gets in the way, slows you down. Instead you invited me here, but told me to keep who I was a secret. I heard someone say: you think you can see what people are like. Now look again. Try to see why — something like that. Suddenly, they stopped being silly caricatures and became real people with real struggles, who are only trying to do their best. I looked round, and I was in a room full of mirrors. I looked and I was Robyn, ambitious, impatient, convinced I knew best. I looked again. I was Caro, always putting my faith in the wrong person, still afraid of the dark, of the doubt. I was Ann, trying to ignore what I really feel inside, trying too hard to be everything to everyone... when I could have been like Kat, terrified of rejection but prepared to risk everything to change; like Patricia, trusting the choice I'd made, trusting God to make it all come right. It's been amazing, this weekend. I've seen how six strangers can change and grow, by being together. That's what you wanted, wasn't it? By making me a fly on the wall? Not to spy on them but to watch and learn. What an idiot I've been! Trying to do it my way, instead of... So today I'd have to say that what our life, our work is about is learning to live together in harmony, so that together we can hold up our world — our beautiful, broken world — for healing. And ourselves along with it. That's what it means to be a nun. That's what nuns have to teach the world.

Slowly, the group at the back begin to come forward, the increasingly pleading note in their voices contrasting with their slow, deliberate steps downstage. But Kat and Ann do not move

Robyn Take me.
Patricia Please.
Stephanie Take me back.
Caro And me...I think
Ann But not me. Please, not me.
Kat Stop!

Everyone freezes. No one looks at her — after all, these are private interviews which we just happen to be overhearing simultaneously

Kat starts to come forward until she is standing to one side of Stephanie's chair. She looks directly at the panel

Do I still want in? I wasn't sure. Till now. Now I see, my mother was wrong: love isn't love that has to be earned. Love is given freely, to give, freely, to others. I've grown up. I'm not that little girl, afraid of ending up in that long, dark room anymore. Now I want to make sure no one else ends up there either. So, yes. I want in. I want home.

Without taking her eyes off the panel, Stephanie gives Kat's hand a squeeze. Everyone speaks loudly, simultaneously:

All Please!

Black-out

Everyone except Robyn leaves the stage

The lights come up on general lighting

Robyn goes to the table and hesitates. She picks up the last envelope

> *Ann and Caro enter, happily chatting,* UR. *Ann carries a drawing of her group's attempt at Task Two*

Caro Sleep well?
Robyn (*spinning round; guiltily*) When?
Caro Last night, of course.
Ann I did. I woke up this morning feeling really... hopeful.
Robyn I can't think why.
Caro What are you doing?

Robyn ignores her. Ann prattles on, unaware of the growing tension between her two friends

Ann Because I realized something. I've changed. We all have. Before we were just strangers. Now we're friends. Working together. It works. And it's fun. Is that the envelope for our solutions?
Robyn No.
Ann I've finished the drawing. For our group. You know, the pyramid. Patricia said to put it in with theirs. (*Opening the fifth envelope, marked "Your Solutions", and pulling out a piece of paper from inside it*) Oh.
Caro You're very quiet?
Robyn And you're not.
Ann They did a real pyramid.
Caro So did we.
Ann No. We only did a triangle. I knew something was wrong. Oh, well.
Robyn That settles it

Ann I still wonder if teams of four meant teams of four...
Caro What are you up to, Robyn?
Ann It is amazing. 'Cos really we're not a bit alike. Don't have anything in common. Now, we're like... sisters! (*She laughs*)
Robyn We may be sisters now, but in one hour's time, we'll be ——
Caro Rivals? Again?
Robyn (*breaking* c) You don't understand. This is one race I must win!
Caro Even by cheating?
Robyn (*making to open Envelope Four*) Call it insurance.
Ann I'm not sure.
Robyn Well, I am. At school, girls I grew up with, girls who were my friends: I had the looks, I got the boyfriends; they got what I left. Now they're all married. And I get what they left. At work, girls I trained with — girls I trained — they get Heathrow-New York. After six years I'm back to Bradford-Belfast, Bradford-Birmingham, Bradford-London. And all because I biffed a guy in Business.
Ann But, you said ——

Caro raises a hand to silence Ann

Robyn Why do you think I chose a job like this? Because no one else wants it. Like the Civil Service — everyone's last resort! No one else wants me. Made for each other! I'll take it. And this time nothing and no one will stop me! (*She rips open the envelope and reads*) Task Four: "Your fourth task was to help each other succeed in the tasks you were given, including the practical jobs like the cooking and washing up, to see if you could work in a group. In your notebook, record who did what and why some of you did nothing". (*She sits* c)

Ann crosses to the table, deep in thought

   Bugger.
Caro Drat.

Ann Oops.
Robyn
Caro } (*together*) Oops?
Robyn Messed up, again!

Stephanie and Kat enter UR, *laughing. Gloomy faces meet them*

Stephanie Whatever'swrong?
Robyn You've won. (*She hands Kat Task Four*)
Kat (*skimming it*) Oh, for goodness sake! Haven't you realized yet? It's not a competition!
Caro But you did it all.
Kat And you let us.
Robyn There's no need to rub it in!
Kat That's just as important, isn't it? Letting someone love you, letting them show they care — that's just as important as washing a few dishes. And a damn sight harder.
Robyn (*throwing herself, sobbing into Kat's arms*) Oh, Kat, I wish I were like you!
Kat (*being startled; patting her on the back*) There, there...
Robyn Of course, I don't mean your hair. What happened? A hedge-trimmer?
Kat Don't spoil it.
Robyn I need a cigarette.
Kat Sorry. Gave up last night. Threw mine away.

One by one, they collect a pad and pen from Ann and exit thoughtfully CL

Ann picks up a notepad, then throws it away and runs off CL

Robyn, with a flight bag, enters UL, *and Caro trails on behind her, with a holdall and an odd assortment of carrier bags. They are heading, eventually, for* DR

Robyn Bloody cheek!

Caro They said I was having second thoughts.
Robyn You were.
Caro They said people don't come here to escape the world but to engage with it.
Robyn Be grateful. They told me they're not easy pickings, ripe for a takeover. They said my problem is I always see what's wrong, not what's right: what I can get, not what I can give.
Caro That's true. But what does it mean?
Robyn We've been sussed.
Caro Oh, no! Where now?
Robyn (*grimly*) Back to Bradford!
Caro But I don't live in Bradford.
Robyn I do.
Caro I thought you lived in London?
Robyn I did. Till I punched that lecher in Business Class. He got an apology. I got a final warning and a one-way ticket to Bradford.
Caro What about me? I gave in my notice when I was coming here. I thought, they're bound to —
Robyn Oh, do stop snivelling! You can get another job.
Caro But this one gave me a room! Without this job, I have no room — nowhere to go — tonight!
Robyn Come back with me.
Caro You?
Robyn I've got a spare room. You can have that. Tomorrow, I'll take you round the airport hotels. They're always on the lookout for new staff. Get you fixed up in no time.
Caro They don't have live-in staff, not at those kind of——
Robyn Haven't I said? You'll move in with me.
Caro But I can't cook.
Robyn You can learn. We can both learn. And when we've found you a job, let's see if together we can't find you a boyfriend. One for me as well.
Caro I'll be in your way.
Robyn Caro, I've got friends. Hundreds of friends. I spend my

life on the phone to my friends. But know what? They never ring back. Seems I can make friends. But not keep them. Perhaps we could learn, from each other?

Caro puts an arm round her shoulder. They continue on their way to DR

Ann enters CL *with an old tartan suitcase. She looks totally dazed and throughout this Scene is deep in thought*

Sorry, Ann. Can we give you a lift?
Ann No, thanks. My father is coming for me.
Caro Best of luck.
Ann I won't need luck. That's something I'm definitely taking away with me from this weekend. A mind of my own.
Caro Robyn, are you sure?
Robyn Come on, *caro mio*. Time to go home.

Ann sits C *and waits happily*

Caro and Robyn exit DR. *Pause. Kat and Patricia enter* CR

Kat I don't believe it!
Patricia So you said.
Kat I still don't believe it!
Patricia It's true. We're going to be sisters!

They embrace

Kat They want me! Somebody actually wants me!
Patricia Ann? Are you all right?
Ann Wonderful.
Kat What did they say?
Ann No.
Patricia Oh. I'm... sorry.
Ann I'm not. It was never my idea. My vocation is with children. Maybe, one day, my own children.

Patricia Then I'm happy for you.
Kat But your father?
Ann Don't worry. Things are going to be very different at home from now on.

Stephanie enters UL

Stephanie Good for you.
Kat Well?
Stephanie Welcome to my family. (*The three of them embrace*) What is it they say? If you want to go quickly —
Kat Go it alone.
Stephanie If you want to go far —
Patricia Go together.
Ann Seems that's something we all need to learn.
Patricia 'Bye, Ann.

Patricia and Stephanie head for the exit, UL

Kat (*to Ann*) Good luck. God speed.
Ann Thanks. And you.

They exit UL, *leaving Ann alone*

Ann recognizes someone approaching, DL

Ann (*rising*) Over here, Father. Yes, I'm ready now.

Quick curtain

THE END

FURNITURE AND PROPERTY LIST

On stage: Eight chairs, in a wide semi-circle across C, facing DC
Small table ULC. *On it:* four A4 envelopes, each containing a typed sheet of instructions, and marked Tasks One, Two, Three, Four; a fifth one marked "Your Solutions" and containing a drawing of the triangular-based pyramid solution; at least six pads, six pens

Offstage: Plank (**Kat**)
Plate of sandwiches (**Patricia**)
Ancient holdall and collection of plastic bags, all stuffed full, but securely tied (**Caro**)
Old tartan suitcase (**Ann**)
Flight bag on wheels (**Robyn**)
Drawing of her group's attempt at the pyramid (**Ann**)

Personal: **Kat:** packet of cigarettes
Robyn: shiny lighter

LIGHTING PLOT

Main acting areas: ULC, C, DC

Two lighting states: general lighting for group sessions alternating with a pool of cold, bright light in a broad band across C for interview sessions.

To open: Black-out. Count three. Snap on interview lighting

Cue 1	**Stephanie:** "Will someone please tell me what this is all about!" *Quick cross-fade to general lighting*	(Page 3)
Cue 2	**Robyn:** "Last night a bit hazy..." *Quick cross-fade to interview lighting*	(Page 4)
Cue 3	**Kat:** "Why don't they just get on with it!" *Quick cross-fade to general lighting*	(Page 4)
Cue 4	**Robyn:** "Oh, really! What for this time?" *Quick cross-fade to interview lighting*	(Page 9)
Cue 5	**Ann:** "Can I go now, please?" *Quick cross-fade to general lighting*	(Page 10)
Cue 6	**Robyn:** "That's it! The place is bugged!" *Quick cross-fade to interview lighting*	(Page 12)
Cue 7	**Caro:** "I can start tomorrow." **Robyn** laughs *Quick cross-fade to general lighting*	(Page 14)

Lighting Plot

Cue 8	**Ann:** "I'm not sure I do. Not sure I can. Oh, decisions, decisions!" *Quick cross-fade to interview lighting*	(Page 20)
Cue 9	**Stephanie:** "Enough! I can't go on with this — not any more!" *Quick cross-fade to general lighting*	(Page 21)
Cue 10	**Ann:** "Steph? They want you. No, just you." *Quick cross-fade to interview lighting*	(Page 28)
Cue 11	**All:** "Please!" *Black-out*	(Page 30)
Cue 12	**Everyone** leaves the stage except **Robyn** who goes to the table *Bring up general lighting*	(Page 30)

EFFECTS PLOT

No sound effects or music in this play

www.ingramcontent.com/pod-product-compliance
Lightning Source LLC
Chambersburg PA
CBHW070637050426
42450CB00011B/3234